The Role of a Chiropractor In Treating Auto Accident Injuries

By Jason A. Plotkin, Esq.

Chief Executive Officer
Pinder Plotkin LLC
www.PinderPlotkin.com
(410) 661-9440

Accepting Refferals for Personal Injury & Workers' Compensation Cases <u>NATIONWIDE</u>
(410) 661-9440 or jplotkin@pinderplotkin.com

National Speaker on Personal Injury & Workers' Compensation Topics
Check availability to speak at your organization
(410) 661-9440 or marketing@pinderplotkin.com

Copyright © Jason A. Plotkin 2019
ALL RIGHTS RESERVED

Table of Contents

Chapter One
First Steps After a Motor Vehicle Accident 1

Chapter Two
Goals of Chiropractic Care After a Motor Vehicle Accident 4

Chapter Three
Common Injuries Treated by Chiropractors 8

Chapter Four
What Will the First Visit Be Like?..14

Chapter Five
Goals of Chiropractic Care After a Motor Vehicle Accident ...18

Chapter Six
What Methods are Used by Chiropractors to Treat Traffic Accident Victims? 22

Chapter Seven
Side Effects and Benefits of Chiropractic Care After a Car Accident 26

Chapter Eight
Qualifications of A Chiropractor in Maryland........................31

The information provided in this book is provided for informational purposes only, and should not be construed as legal advice on any subject. No attorney-client relationship is formed until a case is accepted by an attorney and a fee agreement is signed.

About the Author

So I am a lawyer. Why should you care? Yes, it's my vocation, but besides that I'm just like you. I have a family, a wife and two children. Every day I go out into the world to provide for them, I come home and have fun with them and I worry about them. In my free time I love to cook and I have two fantasy football teams that take up way too much of my free time, but I can also claim four championships!! If you are going to be distracted at least make it worth your while.

So yes, I am a lawyer, but I practice for three reasons: to **love**, to **serve** and to **care**. If you can get those three things right in any occupation you have, then everyone else wins. That's the goal. And after all isn't that what life is all about?

I fight for the rights of injury vicitims everyday and see the great treatment AND results that chiropractors provide to clients injured in auto accidents (motor vehcile collisions). I had the privilege of presenting AutoComp (auto accident in the course of employment) at the Maryland Chiropractic Association's Spring 2017 Forum.

In 2018, I was honored to be certified as a life member of the Million Dollar Advocates Forum. The Million Dollar Advocates Forum is recognized as one of the most prestigious groups of trial lawyers in the United States. Membership is limited to attorneys who have won million and multi-million-dollar verdicts, awards and settlements.

I am a regular presenter at personal injury and workers' compensation continuing legal education classes.

Awards & Accolades

2019: The National Trial Lawyers: Top 100 Civil Plaintiffs Lawyers

2019: Lawyers of Distinction: Workers' Compensation Law

2018: Million Dollar Advocates Forum

2018: Outstanding Leadership Award, Parkville Carney Business Association

2017: The Honorable John Sarbanes, Outstanding Volunteer Service to the Business and Community of Parkville and surrounding communities

2017: Baltimore County Executive, Kevin Kamenetz, Executive Citation, Recognized for Commitment to the Residents of Baltimore County

2017: The Maryland General Assembly Citation, Outstanding Volunteer Service to the Residents of Baltimore County

2017: Baltimore County Council Resolution, Recognized for Commitment to the Residents of Baltimore County

2016: SmartCEO Centers of Influence Award

2016: The Daily Record's VIP List, Successful Before 40

2016: Baltimore County Council Resolution, Outstanding Volunteer Award with the Parkville Carney Business Association

2016: Maryland General Assembly Citation, Outstanding Volunteer Services to Parkville, Carney and surrounding communities

2016: The Senate of Maryland Citation, Outstanding Volunteer Service at the Parkville Carney Business Association

2016: Baltimore County Executive, Kevin Kamenetz, Executive Citation, Recognized for Commitment to the People of Baltimore County

2015 : Governor Larry Hogan, Jr., State of Maryland, Governor's Volunteer Certificate

2015 : Baltimore County Executive, Kevin Kamenetz, Executive Citation, Best Advocate Parkville Commercial District

2015 : Baltimore County Council Resolution, 2015 Parkville Towne Center Fair Volunteer Award

2015 : The Senate of Maryland Citation, Outstanding Volunteer Service to the Businesses and Citizens of the Parkville Community

2015 : The Maryland General Assembly Citation, Outstanding Volunteer Service to the Business and Community of Parkville and surrounding communities

2015 : Baltimore County Department of Planning Nominee, Best District Advocate

2014 : The Parkville Carney Business Association, Inc., Certificate of Service & Commitment

2014 : Baltimore County Council Resolution, Honored for service in the community

2014 : The Senate of Maryland, Honored for service in the community

2014 : The Maryland General Assembly, Honored for service in the community

Chapter One
First Steps After a Motor Vehicle Accident

According to the National Highway Traffic Safety Administration (NHTSA), nearly 7.3 million accidents were reported in 2016.[1] As a result of those traffic accidents, over 3.1 million people were injured, and 37,461 people were killed. The number of traffic accidents increased in 2016 by almost one million crashes.

Each day in the United States, thousands of individuals are injured in motor vehicle accidents, including pedestrians and bicyclists. When an individual is injured in a collision, it is very important for that person to take certain steps to protect his or her health. It is also important to take steps to protect a person's legal rights to file an accident claim against the responsible party.

Actions to Take After a Traffic Accident

Before we discuss chiropractic care after a car accident, we want to review the steps you should take following any traffic accidents.

➲ **Call 911 immediately!** Regardless of the severity of a crash, you need to report the accident to the police. It is

---

[1] National Center for Statistics and Analysis. (2018, September). Summary of motor vehicle crashes: 2016 data. (Traffic Safety Facts. Report No. DOT HS 812 580). Washington, DC: National Highway Traffic Safety Administration

extremely important for you to have an official record of the accident.

- **Document the accident scene.** If you can do so without placing yourself or others in harm, you should make a video of the accident scene and take pictures of the scene. You need to include images of all vehicles involved in the crash and the area surrounding the vehicles, especially road signs and traffic signals.
- **Gather information from witnesses.** If there are eyewitnesses at the scene, you need to ask each witness for his or her name and contact information. Eyewitness testimony can be extremely valuable if the other driver denies liability for the crash.
- **Make notes.** While you are waiting for the police to arrive, you should also try to make a few notes while the memory of the accident is fresh on your mind. What do you remember immediately prior to the crash? Did the other driver say anything after the collision?
- **Avoid admitting fault.** When the police officer arrives at the accident scene, you need to provide accurate information about the cause of the accident, but you should not admit fault or say you are sorry. Admitting fault could prevent you from receiving the medical care you need, including chiropractic care.
- **Seek medical attention for your injuries.** If you did not go to the emergency room directly from the crash scene, you should see a doctor as soon as possible after the traffic accident. A delay in treatment can cause additional health problems. Furthermore, a delay in treatment could jeopardize your ability to receive

compensation for your injuries, including reimbursement for chiropractic care after a car accident.

⮕ **Continue seeking care from a health care provider.** Even though you might "feel better," you should not stop treatment until your doctor releases you. This step is important for your health and your accident claim.

An Important Final Step to Protect Yourself and Your Family

Another important step that you should take after a traffic accident is to learn about your legal rights. Filing an insurance claim can be a challenging process, especially for an accident victim who is continuing to recover after an accident. Instead of dealing with the stress of the claims process, you should contact an attorney to discuss your case.

In the following chapters of this book, we discuss chiropractic care and how it helps individuals heal after a traffic-related injury.

Chapter Two
Goals of Chiropractic Care After a Motor Vehicle Accident

Your goal in visiting a chiropractor (DC) and embarking on a chiropractic treatment plan is usually to relieve pain. Your chiropractor has that same goal; however, he or she also has several other chiropractic goals that can benefit you in the long-term.

Your DC's goal is to realign and treat your conditions through nonsurgical, drug-free manual manipulations to allow your body to heal naturally. With that in mind, chiropractic care has several short-term and long-term goals for your overall health and well-being.

Short-Term Chiropractic Goals

The short-term chiropractic goals are usually straightforward. The DC wants to reduce or alleviate the pain you are experiencing from the car accident by realignment of your spine. In addition, through adjustments and hand manipulation, the chiropractor seeks to restore normal joint function and muscle balance. Through ongoing chiropractic treatments, your body can begin to heal itself so that you feel better and stronger.

Long-Term Goals of Chiropractic Care

The purpose of your chiropractic care is to focus on your long-term goals in addition to the short-term goal of relieving pain. Your DC will also focus on improving your tolerance to normal daily activities to help you get back to a normal routine after sustaining injuries in a car accident.

Restoring functional independence is an important goal for long-term health and well-being. While it is important to relieve pain to encourage you to remain active, it is also important to address any underlying problems that could limit or hinder your ability to recover fully from car accident injuries.

Three Goals of a Chiropractic Treatment Plan

There are three main goals of any chiropractic treatment plan:

❖ **Pain Reduction**

During the initial phase of your treatment plan, the goal is to reduce your pain level. Most car accident victims visit a chiropractor because they are in pain. In some cases, a patient may visit a DC because the painkillers prescribed by a physician are not working, or they do not like how the painkillers make them feel. While every patient is different, many patients experience a reduction in pain within two weeks.

If continued chiropractic care does not significantly reduce pain, further evaluation and modification of the treatment plan might be necessary. In some cases, a chiropractor refers a patient for additional testing and treatment if the chiropractic treatments are not providing the relief expected.

❖ Improving Function

During the next phase of your treatment plan, after your pain has been reduced, it is time to work on restoring your flexibility and strength. The goal of restoring flexibility and strength is to improve the function of your neuromuscular skeleton. The DC wants to bring you to the point of performing most normal daily activities without aggravating your symptoms. While working to improve function, you work with your chiropractor as a team with the goal of improving your health. The number of visits to your DC may decrease as you continue with a home exercise program recommended by the DC to continue to improve your balance, strength, and function.

❖ Maintaining Health

Your chiropractor wants to help you maintain your health after you have recovered from the injuries sustained in a car accident. During the Wellness Phase of your chiropractic care, your DC works with you to help you continue the good health and wellness you achieved during the first two phases of your chiropractic treatment plan. Your chiropractor provides routine examinations to check for muscle and joint dysfunction that, if left untreated, may result in serious problems that could impact your work, daily activities, and lifestyle. After working diligently to heal from car accident injuries, you want to continue the investment in your health by receiving regular wellness care.

As you are taking steps to recover from your injuries, an insurance adjuster may pressure you to settle your accident claim. It is **_not_** in your best interest to settle a claim until you understand the full extent of your injuries, including any permanent impairments or disabilities. While you focus on recovery, your lawyer will focus on protecting your legal rights and reducing the stress of dealing with an accident claim.

Chapter Three
Common Injuries Treated by Chiropractors

Many accident victims consult chiropractors (DCs) because chiropractors treat a broad range of conditions and injuries that are common in motor vehicle accidents. Unlike other healthcare professionals who prescribe painkillers to deal with car accident injuries, a DC can use a variety of chiropractic methods to correct spinal misalignments to promote natural healing without the use of drugs or invasive treatments.

Common Traffic Accident Injuries Treated with Chiropractic Care

Three of the common auto accident injuries that chiropractors treat without surgery or drugs include:

> **WHIPLASH AND OTHER NECK INJURIES**

Whiplash is a common injury in traffic accidents, especially rear-end collisions and head-on crashes. When a person's neck is whipped backward and forward in a violent manner, as in a car crash, it can cause damage to the soft tissues (ligaments and muscles) of the neck. When the ligaments and muscles extend beyond the normal range of motion, small tears can develop.

In some cases, an accident victim may not realize he or she has whiplash for several days or weeks when the symptoms persist or become worse. Symptoms of whiplash include[2]:

- Neck pain, especially when turning the head to look over a shoulder
- Headaches
- Blurred vision
- Shoulder pain
- Dizziness
- Arm pain
- Pain in the lower back
- Stiff neck
- Reduced range of motion in the neck, shoulders, or upper arms

If whiplash is not treated correctly, the injury may continue to cause severe pain and limit the range of motion for years. Sadly, some physicians do not treat cases of whiplash seriously enough. They prescribe pain medications and rest. As the injury heals, scarring develops causing limited range of motion if the spine is not aligned before the scar tissue develops.

Chiropractic care helps relieve pain, restore mobility, and allows long-term healing without drugs. DCs may use a combination of chiropractic methods to treat whiplash, including spinal adjustments, rehabilitative exercises, and electric muscle stimulation. Because chiropractors have extensive experience treating soft tissue injuries and dealing with injuries that other doctors simply "medicate" instead of treating, a chiropractor can be the one health care

---

[2] Mayo Clinic (https://www.mayoclinic.org/diseases-conditions/whiplash/symptoms-causes/syc-20378921)

professional who listens to your complaints and takes your symptoms seriously.

> **BACK INJURIES**

Back injuries are also common in car accidents, especially low back injuries. Many accident victims suffer back pain from sprained backs, herniated discs, fractured vertebrae, or broken vertebrae. The impact of a vehicle crash can cause severe damage to the soft tissues of the spine. The trauma to the soft tissues causes pain, limited mobility, tension, and irritation.

Herniated discs are a common back injury that chiropractors treat after car accidents. The herniated disc causes pressure on the spinal cord nerves which can cause weakness, pain, or numbness. A DC uses flexion-distraction, manual therapy, spinal manipulation, pelvic blocking, therapeutic exercises, and other chiropractic methods to treat herniated discs.

Back pain can be debilitating. The pain can prevent you from working or enjoying normal daily activities. It is very important to see a medical professional if you experience any symptoms of spinal cord injuries or back injuries after an accident. Symptoms of spinal cord injuries and back injuries include[3]:

- Pain in the back or pressure in the head, back, or neck
- Difficulty with walking or balance
- Paralysis in any body part
- Lack of coordination or weakness

---

[3] Mayo Clinic (https://www.mayoclinic.org/diseases-conditions/spinal-cord-injury/symptoms-causes/syc-20377890)

- Tingling, numbness, or loss of sensation in toes, feet, fingers, or hands
- Difficulty breathing
- Loss of bladder or bowel control
- Twisted or oddly positioned back or neck

A back injury or spinal cord injury may not always be noticed right away after a motor vehicle accident. However, a delay in treatment could cause additional injuries and adverse conditions. It is best to see a healthcare professional after any car accident for diagnostic tests and evaluation.

> **PINCHED NERVES**

Pinched nerves usually occur in the spine after a car accident, but you can experience a pinched nerve anywhere throughout your body. When a nerve is pinched, there is increased pressure on that nerve causing pain, numbness, and tingling. Pinched nerves can develop in conjunction with whiplash and other spinal cord injuries, including herniated discs.

Chiropractors treat pinched nerves in several ways, including manual spinal adjustments. Through manual adjustments, the never endings relax and can return to the correct position to alleviate pain and other symptoms.

Symptoms of pinched nerves include[4]:

- Tingling or "pins and needles" sensations

---

[4] Mayo Clinic (https://www.mayoclinic.org/diseases-conditions/pinched-nerve/symptoms-causes/syc-20354746)

- Decreased sensation or numbness in the area supplied by the nerve
- Muscle weakness
- Aching, sharp, or burning pain that can radiate outward from the area
- Feeling like your foot or hand has "fallen asleep"

Many doctors prescribe rest and painkillers for pinched nerves. However, if the source of the problem is not treated, a pinched nerve can cause long-term health problems. Chiropractors do not merely treat the symptoms, they address the cause of the symptoms to provide overall healing and improved health.

Other Common Injuries Chiropractors Treat After a Car Accident

In addition to the above injuries, there are several other soft tissue injuries that chiropractors treat after a motor vehicle accident including:

- Coccydynia
- Sciatica
- Degenerative disc disorder
- Cerviogenic headache
- Subluxation
- Spinal osteoarthritis
- Tendonitis

The above list is not an exhaustive list of injuries from car accidents that chiropractic care may treat. A DC will perform several tests and a full examination to determine the correct diagnosis and treatment plan for your car accident injuries.

Medical bills from DCs and other health care providers can easily reach into the thousands of dollars. Lawyers will assist clients in documenting all medical expenses and costs so they can seek reimbursement for these expenses from the party responsible for their injuries.

Chapter Four
What Will the First Visit Be Like?

Many people have never visited a chiropractor (DC) before an auto accident, so they do not know what to expect during their first visit. Your first visit with a DC is much like the first visit with any other healthcare professional. The first step is to review your symptoms and history with the chiropractor before moving to a physical examination and diagnosis.

Initial Consultation to Review Symptoms and Patient History

This portion of your chiropractic visit will be like visiting a family doctor for the first time. The chiropractor needs to obtain a detailed description of the symptoms you are experiencing in addition to obtaining a complete record of your health and medical care history. The information may be obtained in several ways, including questionnaires, discussions with medical assistants, and discussions with the DC. Information you can expect to provide may include:

- General personal information (i.e. name, address, contact information, etc.)
- Description of symptoms and when they began
- A brief description of the motor vehicle accident
- A detailed health history, including any surgeries, medical procedures, past injuries, allergies, etc.

It is essential that you are honest and thorough in your responses to the chiropractor's questions. This information assists the DC in diagnosing the problem and developing a successful treatment plan. However, you should consult an attorney before providing a written or verbal description of the motor vehicle accident. What you say in your statement could help or hurt your claim. Most lawyers will provide free consultations for accident victims so they can learn about the claims process and receive support and assistance as they continue with their medical treatment.

The Chiropractic Examination

After completing the initial paperwork and history, the chiropractor conducts a physical examination. The examination consists of gathering general data, such as your weight, pulse, blood pressure, height, and oxygen level. However, it also includes specific tests that focus on the area of the body where you are experiencing symptoms.

Depending on the symptoms and the affected area, a DC may perform tests to determine:

- Range of motion
- Muscle strength
- Posture analysis
- Neurological integrity
- Diagnostic tests, if necessary, including MRI scan, x-rays, CT scan, and laboratory tests

The DC may also perform chiropractic manipulation of the sore area to gather additional information. After a comprehensive examination and completion of required diagnostic tests, the chiropractor can provide a diagnosis and treatment plan.

Diagnosis and Treatment Plan

Once a DC completes the patient history, physical examination, and diagnostic tests, he or she can make a diagnosis based on the information gathered from all sources. The chiropractor will explain the problems and issues discovered during the examination and whether chiropractic care is recommended. The DC also explains why and how chiropractic care can help you recover and heal from injuries sustained in the car accident.

After discussing the results of the examination and the diagnosis, the DC reviews the prescribed chiropractic treatment plan. During this discussion, you should ask questions and raise concerns that you feel need to be addressed before moving forward with treatment. When you complete the first visit, you should have the following information:

- A detailed diagnosis of your condition;
- Individualized chiropractic treatment plan tailored to treat your specific injuries and conditions;
- Explanation of methods and treatment options;

- Risks and benefits of the prescribed treatment plan; and,
- Anticipated length of treatment and chiropractic care to correct the problems.

If the chiropractor did not provide a written summary of your visit, you should request the summary for your records.

Documenting your recovery is an important step in the accident claims process. The more information, evidence, and details you have about your recovery, the better chance you have of recovering maximum compensation. However, documenting losses and damages during your recovery may feel overwhelming. Your attorney can help you with this step so that you can focus more on your health.

Chapter Five
Goals of Chiropractic Care After a Motor Vehicle Accident

Your goal in visiting a chiropractor (DC) and embarking on a chiropractic treatment plan is usually to relieve pain. Your chiropractor has that same goal; however, he or she also has several other chiropractic goals that can benefit you in the long-term.

Your DC's goal is to realign and treat your conditions through nonsurgical, drug-free manual manipulations to allow your body to heal naturally. With that in mind, chiropractic care has several short-term and long-term goals for your overall health and well-being.

Short-Term Chiropractic Goals

The short-term chiropractic goals are usually straightforward. The DC wants to reduce or alleviate the pain you are experiencing from the car accident by realignment of your spine. In addition, through adjustments and hand manipulation, the chiropractor seeks to restore normal joint function and muscle balance. Through ongoing chiropractic treatments, your body can begin to heal itself so that you feel better and stronger.

Long-Term Goals of Chiropractic Care

Restoring functional independence is an important goal for long-term health and well-being. While it is important to relieve pain to encourage you to remain active, the purpose of your chiropractic care is to focus on your long-term goals in addition to the short-term goal of relieving pain. Your DC will also focus on improving your tolerance to normal daily activities to help you get back to a normal routine after sustaining injuries in a car accident.

It is also important to address any underlying problems that could limit or hinder your ability to recover fully from car accident injuries.

Three Goals of a Chiropractic Treatment Plan

There are three main goals of any chiropractic treatment plan:

❖ **Pain Reduction**

During the initial phase of your treatment plan, the goal is to reduce your pain level. Most car accident victims visit a chiropractor because they are in pain. In some cases, a patient may visit a DC because the painkillers prescribed by a physician are not working, or they do not like how the painkillers make them feel. While every patient is different, many patients experience a reduction in pain within two weeks.

If continued chiropractic care does not significantly reduce pain, further evaluation and modification of the treatment plan might be necessary. In some cases, a chiropractor refers a patient for additional testing and treatment if the chiropractic treatments are not providing the relief expected.

❖ Improving Function

During the next phase of your treatment plan, after your pain has been reduced, it is time to work on restoring your flexibility and strength. The goal of restoring flexibility and strength is to improve the function of your neuromuscular skeleton. The DC wants to bring you to the point of performing most normal daily activities without aggravating your symptoms. While working to improve function, you work with your chiropractor as a team with the goal of improving your health. The number of visits to your DC may decrease as you continue with a home exercise program recommended by the DC to continue to improve your balance, strength, and function.

❖ Maintaining Health

Your chiropractor wants to help you maintain your health after you have recovered from the injuries sustained in a car accident. During the Wellness Phase of your chiropractic care, your DC works with you to help you continue the good health and wellness you achieved during the first two phases of your chiropractic treatment plan. Your chiropractor provides routine examinations to check for muscle and joint dysfunction that, if left untreated, may result in serious problems that could impact your work, daily activities, and lifestyle. After working diligently to heal from car accident injuries, you want to continue the investment in your health by receiving regular wellness care.

It is during this phase of treatment that many accident victims realize they need assistance from an attorney. They may be dealing with unpaid medical bills, lost income, and pressure from an insurance adjuster.

Chapter Six
What Methods are Used by Chiropractors to Treat Traffic Accident Victims?

Doctors of Chiropractic (DCs) are trained to use several different techniques and methods to treat patients suffering from car accident injuries. Because some techniques may not work for every patient, a chiropractor develops a chiropractic treatment plan that is best suited to offer the patient the best chance of recovering from car accident injuries while improving spinal mobility, decreasing pain, improving range of motion, and improving overall general health.

There are numerous techniques, methods, and forms of chiropractic treatment. Below are some of the more common methods used by DCs to treat car accident victims.

Common Techniques and Treatments Used by Chiropractors to Treat Car Accident Injuries

Chiropractic Adjustment

Chiropractic adjustment or spinal manipulation[5] is one of the most common methods used by DCs to treat their patients. This treatment method is the method that most people associate with chiropractors as the "cracking your back" method of chiropractic care. A DC does not "crack" your

---
[5] Chiropractic Treatments for Lower Back Pain. Steven G. Yeomans DC. Spine-Health.com. 14 March 2013.

back, but you might hear a sound similar to a crack that is known as joint cavitation.

The "crack" occurs when the DC applies pressure as he maneuvers specific vertebrae that are misaligned or functioning improperly. Spinal manipulation is often used to treat joint pain and lower back pain.

Cervical Adjustment

For headaches and neck pain, the chiropractor may perform cervical manual traction[6]. As the DC massages your neck, he uses gentle pressure to stretch your neck as he massages the neck in all directions (up, down, side-to-side, back, and forth). DCs use various techniques and various amounts of pressure to tailor the treatment to the patient's needs.

Traction

Traction[7] can be used to treat general back pain, joint pain, and pain from a herniated disc. This chiropractic method is also used to treat degenerative discs and to correct posture. The chiropractor manually applies force and pressure to the patient's limbs, head, or back. In some cases, the DC may use a wedge or other tool to assist with this treatment. A patient's weight might be used for traction in a treatment known as inversion therapy. Inversion therapy has many pros and cons, and some DCs do not advocate for this method of treatment. You should discuss inversion therapy at great

---

[6] American Chiropractic Association (https://www.acatoday.org/Patients/Health-Wellness-Information/Neck-Pain-and-Chiropractic)
[7] Spinal Traction. Heaven Stubblefield (reviewed by William Morrison, MD). Healthline.com. 11 October 2016.

length with your DC, including the benefits and potential risks.[8]

Other Forms of Chiropractic Care

In some cases, a DC may use physiological therapeutic methods[9] in conjunction with chiropractic methods to treat patients. Some methods a chiropractor may use include:

- Massage — Massage is used to help improve circulation and reduce inflammation and swelling.
- Hot and Cold Therapy — This type of treatment can assist with general back pain, swelling, and improved blood flow. The DC alternates between ice packs and a heating pad, or other forms of hot and cold therapy, which can also increase the healing process.
- Exercise — Your DC may prescribe an exercise program to assist in the healing process and promote general health. Exercises can focus on several different areas and goals, including strengthening and stretching the back.
- Weight Management and Dietary Management — In some cases, a patient may benefit from a weight and dietary management program. The chiropractor may provide information on various programs and dietary restrictions that can help improve joint, muscle, and back health as well as overall general health.

---

[8] What Are the Risks and Benefits of Inversion Therapy? Kristeen Cherney (reviewed by Gregory Minnis, DPT). Healthline.com. 17 March 2017.
[9] Chiropractic Services Beyond Adjustments. Steven G. Yeomans DC. Spine-Health.com. 15 March 2013.

Informed and Prepared

As with any other form of medical treatment, you need to feel comfortable with your choice of chiropractic care. You should ask as many questions as you need to ask to understand the pros and cons of chiropractic care fully. If necessary, you can seek a second opinion before beginning a chiropractic treatment plan.

In our next chapter, we discuss the benefits and risks of chiropractic care, including any potential side effects from chiropractic treatment.

Chapter Seven
Side Effects and Benefits of Chiropractic Care After a Car Accident

There is much debate on the effectiveness and safety of chiropractic care. Below is a brief discussion of the potential benefits and risks associated with chiropractic care according to several sources.

Potential Benefits of Chiropractic Care

There are several benefits[10] that chiropractic care can offer including[11]:

- ☑ **Catches Injuries That Are Not Obvious**

Some injuries sustained in a car accident are not always apparent. Broken bones, lacerations, and fractures are easy to diagnose. However, whiplash, spinal cord injuries, and dislocated discs may not be immediately known following a car accident. It could take days or weeks for symptoms to manifest. The soreness and pain an accident victim experiences may be ignored because it is assumed these symptoms will "go away" once the impact of the collision subsides.

However, these symptoms could indicate a severe injury that, if ignored, could cause long-term adverse health

---

[10] Palmer College of Chiropractic (http://www.palmer.edu/about-us/benefits-of-chiropractic/)
[11] Live Strong (https://www.livestrong.com/article/144502-benefits-of-chiropractic-care/)

consequences. Chiropractors can diagnose these injuries early so that a chiropractic treatment plan can be developed to reduce the risk of long-term damage while speeding the healing process.

☑ Pain Relief Without Medication

Painkillers can have serious side effects and addictive qualities. Furthermore, pain medication does not "treat" the condition, but it merely masks a symptom (pain) of the condition. Many traffic accident victims are prescribed pain medication, but once they stop taking the medication, they realize the pain continues. In some cases, the pain has increased.

Chiropractic care treats the cause of the pain to reduce and alleviate pain caused by car accident injuries. Through a comprehensive chiropractic treatment plan, your DC can relieve pain without the use of addictive medications and dangerous drugs. Chiropractic care heals the underlying injuries instead of masking the pain with drugs.

☑ Non-Invasive Treatment for Car Accident Injuries

Many of the treatments prescribed by other medical providers include invasive surgical procedures that carry the risk of additional injuries and complications. Chiropractic care is a completely non-invasive form of treatment for injuries sustained in a car accident. By using various methods, a chiropractor can realign the spine and joints to reduce pain. In addition, realignment promotes faster healing and general health without the need for surgery.

☑ **Reduction of Inflammation**

X-rays and other diagnostic tests generally do not reveal the microscopic tears in the muscles and ligaments that are often caused by a motor vehicle crash. These tears are one of the reasons accident victims suffer severe pain in the days and weeks following the collision. A DC can use manipulation and other chiropractic techniques to realign the spinal cord, which relieves pain and reduces inflammation by releasing the body's own anti-inflammatory properties.

☑ **Reduction of Scar Tissue**

One of the problems many accident victims experience is the formation of scar tissue. The body's natural healing process causes scar tissue to form around tendons, ligaments, and muscles that have been injured. As the scar tissue forms, it can cause stiffness and become uncomfortable for the patient. A DC can target specific areas to break up scar tissues and promote healing before the scar tissue can fully form. Without scar tissue, injuries can heal properly so that the patient feels better and avoids long-term issues caused by scar tissue.

☑ **Restore Mobility and Range of Motion**

The soreness and stiffness a person feels after a car accident can limit mobility and range of motion. A lack of blood flow and nutrients in the affected areas can cause inflammation and limit range of motion. Through chiropractic adjustments, a DC can mobilize the spine to increase blood flow and essential nutrients to injured areas, which promotes the natural healing process to increase range of motion and mobility.

☑ Improves Overall Health and Well-being

Chiropractic care is not just about treating a specific injury or area. In addition to treating back injuries, whiplash, and soft tissue injuries caused by car accidents, chiropractic adjustments can improve posture, nerve communication, coordination, blood flow, joint motion, and physical function. It can also reduce tension and stress disorders and relieve other chronic injuries and conditions by promoting the body's natural healing process. The preventative health benefits from regular adjustments and chiropractic care can help your body to continue to function at its best.

Potential Side Effects of Chiropractic Treatments

According to the Mayo Clinic,[12] chiropractic adjustments are safe when licensed and trained professionals perform them. However, there are some risks associated with chiropractic care, including the worsening of a herniated disc, the risk of stroke after neck manipulation, and compression of nerves in the back. While these risks are "overall rare," you should still discuss these risks and any other potential risk with your DC before proceeding with treatment.

Some of the most common adverse effects of chiropractic treatment included fatigue, localized discomfort, and

---

[12] Mayo Clinic (https://www.mayoclinic.org/tests-procedures/chiropractic-adjustment/about/pac-20393513)

dizziness. Numbness and tingling have also been reported, but the rates appear to be low.[13] Again, it is up to patients to discuss the benefits and risks with a chiropractor to make an informed decision whether adjustments and other chiropractic treatments are right for them.

Because some authorities do not recognize chiropractic care as a "legitimate" form of treatment after a car accident, insurance companies often attempt to deny claims involving chiropractic care. Contact an experienced lawyer that understands the various tactics used by insurance companies to try to deny claims.

---

[13] MedScape (https://www.medscape.com/viewarticle/740848_2)

Chapter Eight
Qualifications of A Chiropractor in Maryland

The Maryland State Board of Chiropractic Examiners (SBCE) regulates chiropractic care within the state, including issuing licenses to chiropractors who practice within the state.[14] According to the agency's website, there are no waivers or exceptions to the requirements for a chiropractor license in Maryland.

Requirements to Apply for a Chiropractor License in Maryland

The following criteria must be met before anyone can be licensed to practice in Maryland as a chiropractor:

- Graduate from a CCE approved Chiropractic College approved for Maryland licensure;
- Hold both a Bachelor and Doctor of Chiropractic Degree;
- Received a score of 375 for the Physiotherapy Exam for parts one, two, three, and four;

---

[14] Maryland Department of Health (https://health.maryland.gov/chiropractic/Pages/licensurec.aspx)

- Receipt of a sealed transcript and exam scores by the Board directly from the school and NBCE;
- Submission of a completed application for licensure with the applicable fees ($200 application fee and $300 examination fee);
- A score of 75 percent or higher on the Maryland Jurisprudence Exam; and,
- Pass the Physical Therapy portion of the NBCE exam with a minimum score of 375 to practice Physical Therapy.

Requirements to Apply for a Chiropractor License in Maryland for Currently Licensed Chiropractors from Another State

If a chiropractor has practiced for a minimum of five years in another state, he or she may apply for a Maryland chiropractor license based on his or her credentials. In addition to the completed application and applicable fees, the chiropractor must also:

- Submit letters from two licensed chiropractors recommending the chiropractor for licensure in Maryland;
- Request verification of good practice from your State's Board to be submitted as a sealed document to Maryland's Board;
- Pass each of the SPEC, MD Jurisprudence, and NBCE exams with a score of 75 percent or higher; and,

- Submit the Criminal History Records Check (CHRC) – Fingerprinting Receipt.

Continuing Education Requirements for Chiropractors in Maryland

To renew their license to practice chiropractic care in Maryland, chiropractors must submit satisfactory evidence of the completion of continuing education requirements. All applicants must complete 48 hours of continuing education units within 24 months of the renewal date, including:

- Three hours of training in the area of communicable disease, including HIV/AIDS instruction;
- Five hours of risk management, including one hour on jurisprudence; and,
- Certification of Healthcare Provider Level CPR training from the American Heart Association or the American Red Cross.

Verifying a License or Filing a Complaint

Before seeking treatment from a Maryland chiropractor (DC), you can confirm that the DC is licensed to practice in Maryland by visiting the Board's website www.mdnc.com. You may also file a complaint against a chiropractor by calling the Board Office at 410-764-4726.

Most chiropractors in Maryland provide excellent care to their patients, including victims of motor vehicle accidents. Many DCs work closely with other medical professionals, including referring patients for diagnostic tests such as MRIs and CTs, to ensure that their patients receive the care and treatment they need to recover fully from injuries sustained in a car accident.

If you have completed treatment and have not consulted with an attorney, we strongly encourage you to meet with an experienced attorney before settling your case directly with the insurance company.

An insurance adjuster does not work for you! The adjuster's priority is to protect the best interest of the insurance company by paying as little as possible for your claim.

I work with great attorneys located throughout the country; give me a call @ (410) 661-9440 or e-mail @ jplotkin@pinderplotkin.com if you want a **FREE CONSULTATION -- Get The No Fee Guarantee**[SM]

PRACTICE AREAS

Auto Accidents

Motorcycle Accidents

Truck Accidents

Uber & Lyft Accidents

Medical Malpractice

Birth Injuries

Worker's Compensation

Free Consultations
Get The No Fee Guarantee[SM]

(410) 661-9440
or jplotkin@pinderplotkin.com

Visit my website for more information about me and my firm
www.PinderPlotkin.com   www.JasonPlotkin.com

Check out my chiropractic video series on YouTube
(Pinder Plotkin) https://bit.ly/2KdTx58

Like what you've read? Check out our weekly blog series @
www.PinderPlotkin.com/blog

E-Mail marketing@pinderplotkin.com to inquire about Jason A. Plotkin, Esq.'s availability to speak at your next event.

www.ingramcontent.com/pod-product-compliance
Lightning Source LLC
Chambersburg PA
CBHW021848220426
43663CB00005B/455